S0-ARX-919

START-UP
RELIGION

THE JEWISH FAITH

Ruth Nason

CHERRYTREE BOOKS

Distributed in the United States by
Cherrytree Books
1980 Lookout Drive
North Mankato, MN 56001

U.S. publication copyright © Cherrytree Books 2005
International copyright reserved in all countries. No part
of this book may be reproduced in any form without
written permission from the publisher.

Library of Congress Cataloging-in-Publication Data
applied for.

First Edition
9 8 7 6 5 4 3 2 1

First published in 2004 by
Evans Brothers Limited
2A Portman Mansions
Chiltern Street
London W1U 6NR
Copyright © Evans Brothers Limited 2004

Conceived and produced by

White-Thomson Publishing Ltd.

Consultants: Jean Mead, Senior Lecturer in Religious
Education, School of Education, University of
Hertfordshire; Dr Anne Punter, Partnership Tutor,
School of Education, University of Hertfordshire.
Designer: Carole Binding

Picture Acknowledgments:
The Bridgeman Art Library (private collection): page 20
(Marc Chagall: Moses holding up the tablets before the
People of Israel, illustration from 'The Story of Exodus'
published 1966, color litho).
All other photographs by Chris Fairclough.

Cover: All photographs by Chris Fairclough

Printed in China.

Acknowledgments:
Special thanks to the Skillman and Wise families for their
help and involvement in the preparation of this book.

Contents

Different Days

Samuel, Rebecca, and their mom and dad belong to the Jewish faith.

▲ Here they are at home on a Tuesday.

belong   Jewish   faith

▼ Here they are on a Friday evening. What is different in this picture from the one on page 4?

Every Friday evening Jewish people light two candles and have a special meal, with bread called hallah.
It is the beginning of the Jewish holy day called Shabbat.

candles   hallah   holy   Shabbat   5
....

Shabbat Begins

Here is what happens in Samuel's and Rebecca's home each Friday evening.

▶ Mom lights the candles.

▼ Everyone joins in a prayer to welcome in Shabbat.

Can you see who is wearing a hat?

prayer   welcome

◀ **Dad blesses Rebecca and Samuel.**

▼ **He leads the family in singing a prayer to thank God for wine.**

◀ **Samuel and Rebecca break one of the braided hallah loaves. They share it with the family.**

blesses   God   braided

Keeping Shabbat

Jewish people believe that God has **commanded** them to rest from everyday work on Shabbat.

▼ On Saturday morning many people go to a **synagogue**. This is a building where Jewish people **worship** God.

▲ Saturday afternoon is a family time.

commanded   synagogue   worship

Shabbat ends on Saturday evening. Afterward some people have a ceremony called havdalah.

▶ They light a plaited candle

▼ and they smell some spices.

The smell reminds them of Shabbat.

What smells remind you of special times?

ceremony   havdalah   spices

What Is a Mezuzah?

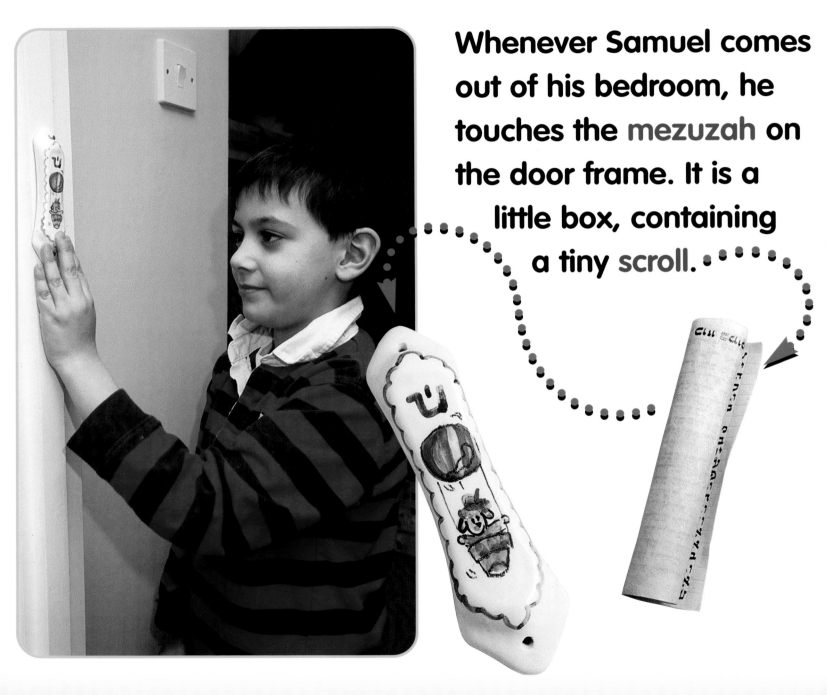

Whenever Samuel comes out of his bedroom, he touches the mezuzah on the door frame. It is a little box, containing a tiny scroll.

mezuzah   scroll

► The writing on the scroll is from the **Bible**. It is in **Hebrew** and is called the **Shema**. It says that the Jewish people should love God and keep his **rules**.

◄ People put mezuzahs on the door frames of their houses, to remind them that God is everywhere.

Bible   **Hebrew**   **Shema**   **rules**

Happy Hanukkah!

Samuel and Rebecca get presents for the festival of
Hanukkah, in December. The festival lasts for eight days.
Can you find out why, from the story on page 13?

festival   Hanukkah   Jerusalem

Long ago, in Jerusalem, the Greek rulers stopped the Jewish people from worshiping God in the Temple. Some brave Jewish soldiers fought the Greeks and won the Temple back.

◄ An oil lamp called a menorah was always kept alight in the Temple. It was a symbol of God being there. When the Jewish people won the Temple back, they found some oil to light the lamp again and a miracle happened. Although there was only enough oil for one day, the lamp stayed alight for eight days, until more oil had been made.

Hanukkah Celebrations

A candleholder called a hanukiah is used at Hanukkah. It has room for eight candles, plus one called the shammas.

▲ On the first evening of Hanukkah Rebecca uses the shammas to light one candle.

▲ On the second evening, Samuel uses the shammas to light two candles.

Guess how many candles they light on the next six evenings.

hanukiah   shammas

▶ Their friends, Joshua and Ethan, are spinning a dreidel.

It has a Hebrew letter on each side. The letters stand for:

great	miracle	happened	here
נ	ג	ה	ש

When the dreidel stops spinning, the boys see which letter is on top. If it is ג or ה , they win chocolate coins.

▶ Which letter can you see on this dreidel?

dreidel

Passover Plate

The Passover festival takes place in spring. There's a special plate of food on the table, for the start of the festival.

Roasted egg

Parsley

Bitter herbs, called maror

Passover   bitter   maror

Roast lamb bone

▼ At Passover, people eat matzo instead of bread. What is the difference?

Haroset, made from apples, nuts, and wine

These foods help people to remember an important time in the history of the Jewish people. See pages 18-19.

matzo   haroset   history   17

The Story of Passover

A book called a haggadah ...... helps people to remember the Passover story. The story begins when the Jewish people were slaves in Egypt.

◀ The bitter herbs on the Passover plate are a reminder of the slaves' hard life.

► Haroset stands for the cement they had to make for the Pharaoh, the king of Egypt.

haggadah   slaves   reminder

God told a man named Moses to say to the Pharaoh, "Let my people go." The Pharaoh said no. God told Moses to say that, if the Pharaoh did not let the people go, God would send ten plagues to punish him. The Pharaoh still said no.

> ▶ Can you find out from the next part of the story what the lamb bone reminds people of?

God said the Jewish people must get ready to leave quickly. Each family must kill a lamb to eat, and put some of its blood on their door frame. That night, the tenth plague happened. All Egyptian first-born sons died, but this plague "passed over" the Jewish homes. The Pharaoh let the Jewish people go.

cement   plagues   first-born

Moses, a Great Leader

The Bible says that God chose Moses to be the leader of the Jewish people. After they left Egypt, God gave Moses rules for the Jewish people to follow.

◀ In this painting, Moses is showing God's rules to the people.

leader

Moses was worried that he would not be able to lead the people, but God said that he would help Moses. What do you think a good leader is like?

fair   strong   brave   calm   wise

In this book you have seen some of the rules that God gave to Moses. Jewish people still follow the rules today.

▼ **Keep Shabbat special.**

▼ **Celebrate Passover every year.**

▲ **Fix a mezuzah on the door frame.**

celebrate

New words introduced in the text:

belong	ceremony	hallah	Jerusalem	Passover	Shema
Bible	commanded	hanukiah	Jewish	plagues	slaves
bitter	dreidel	Hanukkah	leader	prayer	spices
blesses	faith	haroset	maror	reminder	symbol
braided	festival	havdalah	matzo	rules	synagogue
candles	first-born	Hebrew	menorah	scroll	Temple
celebrate	God	history	mezuzah	Shabbat	welcome
cement	haggadah	holy	miracle	shammas	worship

Background Information

The **Jewish religion** dates back to biblical times, but is a living, diverse religion in the "here and now". The family in this book belongs to the Reform movement within Judaism. Care has been taken not to offend the Orthodox Jewish community, although the practices described may differ in some aspects. Try to respect this diversity, e.g. by saying "some Jewish people ...". Also recognize that not all Jewish people practice the religion.

Shabbat runs from Friday sunset to Saturday evening. It begins with lighting candles, representing the two commandments (Exodus 20:8-11 and Deuteronomy 5:12-15), and a celebratory meal where two *hallah* loaves represent the two portions of manna (Exodus 16:1-26). Men and boys and some married women cover their heads as a sign of respect for God.
The "hands in front of the eyes" gesture (page 6) is used only for the Shabbat candle-lighting blessing.
The *havdalah* ceremony says farewell to Shabbat.

Mezuzah cases contain the *Shema*, verses from Deuteronomy 6:4-9, 11:13-21.

The **Hanukkah** story of the Maccabaean revolt is told in the first chapter of 1 Maccabees (in the Apocrypha). The *dreidel* game is said to have originated when Jewish people, forbidden to learn Hebrew, disguised their classes as a game.

The story of **Passover** is in Exodus 12:1-42. *Matzo* is eaten instead of bread. It is a reminder that the Jewish people left Egypt in a hurry; they did not have time to allow their dough to rise and it was baked into flat, unrisen matzo.

Familiar stories of **Moses** are his birth (Exodus 2), the burning bush (Exodus 3), the Exodus (Exodus 5-12), the crossing of the Red Sea (Exodus 14), and the receiving of the ten commandments (Exodus 19 and 20).

Spelling and pronunciation: transliterations of Hebrew words may not match English pronunciation exactly. One Hebrew H is pronounced like the "ch" in "loch" and is written as either H or CH in English. Examples include the initial H in *hallah*, *Hanukkah* and *haroset*.

Parents and Teachers

Suggested Activities

PAGES 4-5

Talk about special meals in the children's lives.
Role-play being guests at a Friday evening meal, using candles, *hallah* loaves, grape juice.

PAGES 6-7

Talk about saying thank you, and the custom of grace before meals. Write "thank-you" cards for the cooks at school or home, with pictures of favorite food.
Tell the story of manna (Exodus 16) in role as a child at the time.

PAGES 8-9

Talk about patterns of work and rest in the children's lives.
Discuss the importance of times to rest and enjoy life.
Make contrasting pictures of weekday and weekend activities.
Make *havdalah* candles: soften wax tapers in warm water and plait them (link to science).

PAGES 10-11

Make a class list of ways to remind ourselves of things we want to remember. Focus on class rules and display them.
Write something that is important to us on stiff paper and roll it into a scroll. Making cases for these can link to science.

PAGES 12-13

Hanukkah can contribute to a cross-curricular topic on light.
Retell the story of the Maccabees, lighting the eight candles of a *hanukiah* (check health and safety aspects).

PAGES 14-15

Make spinning tops with Hebrew letters (or your own alternative) and play a game where children gain or lose one or more counters or (wrapped) sweets.
Discuss the value of rules in a game and in life.

Recommended Resources

BOOKS

Silverman, Maida. *Festival of Lights: The Story of Hanukkah*. New York: Simon & Schuster, 1999.

WEB SITES

www.askmoses.com (an excellent site for questions and information about the Jewish faith)

www.chsweb.org (links to introductory sites on Judaism, what it's like to be a Jewish child, etc)

www.mnment.com/judaism (a good, wide-ranging introduction to Judaism and Jewish religious observances)

PAGES 16-17

Discuss foods that remind children of a person or an event.
Make Passover plate collages on paper plates.

PAGES 18-19

Use a *haggadah*, a Jewish visitor; or a video of a Jewish family to help you retell the Bible story.
When telling the story of the plagues, let the children dip their little finger in a glass of grape juice (for the wine representing joy) and take out one drop as you name each plague. The Jewish people remember that their rescue was at the cost of others' suffering.

PAGES 20-21

Tell some of the stories of Moses.
Draw pictures of leaders children know. Invite people with responsibilities to be interviewed. Discuss what makes a good leader.
Play a game of "follow the leader."

Index